EARLY RETIREMENT GUIDELINES:
How to retire early and still live a fulfilled life

Seven Strategies to prepare you for retirement
And
Five critical questions to ask before you retire early are stated in this book

Charles M. Cardwell

Table of content

CHAPTER 1:

EARLY RETIREMENT

Early retirement is the practice of quitting a job before the legal retirement age, especially when it comes to favourable financial conditions.

"Some will be required to retire early"

If you lose your job or decide to change careers, early retirement could seem like a smart option.

Nonetheless, it's crucial to balance the benefits and drawbacks.

Spend some time carefully considering your financial situation and how it may impact your way of life.

There may be many solid reasons for you to retire early.

If you don't like your job, want to change your lifestyle, or believe it will be better for your health, it may be an alluring option.

Yet, it's equally necessary to take into account the drawbacks, and there are a few significant ones.
They consist of:

Reduced pension.
As opposed to if you had waited to retire until the usual age, your pension is probably going to be lower.
Unless your employer is providing a much-improved package, that is.

No State Pension immediately.
Typically, you must be 55 years old to begin receiving a workplace pension.
Yet until you reach your state pension age, you won't receive a state pension.

Several businesses will make an effort to include incentives in your early retirement package to make it more appealing.

Depending on the type of employment pension you have, they will provide you with a different incentive.

Defined contribution and defined benefit are the two categories.

Examples of incentives your employer might provide are:
a one-time payment made into your defined contribution pension to increase the value of your benefits, which, if you're in a defined benefit plan, are calculated as though you had worked until your typical retirement age.

You will receive a better pension with either incentive than you may otherwise be eligible for.

You can enquire with your company about the kind of pension you have and the available incentives.

It's simple to let images of the winter sun, days spent in the garden, or extra time with your family influence your decision to retire early.
But what's required is a level mind and a methodical approach.

One excellent idea is a checklist.

Compared to the days when you only received your wage at the end of each month, your overall income is probably going to be much more difficult.

You might receive money from many pensions, savings, benefits, part-time work, and other sources.

To start, total everything up.

Request from your company a sample of the pension you would receive in the event of early retirement.

If you plan to start those early, too, ask your other pensions for a forecast.
Using a personal pension or one from a former workplace as examples.

Make sure they have annual increases if you want to purchase an annuity or will be getting payments from a defined benefit pension.
If they don't, you might wish to save more money or hold off on claiming some pensions for the time being.

Visit the government website to learn more about taxes in retirement.

Determine your monthly obligations and outgoing costs.

Budgeting Tool

If you don't go to work every day, your spending habits will change.

For instance, household expenses could increase even though trip expenses could decrease.

You should also consider losing any employee advantages, such as a free cafeteria, a corporate car, or health insurance.

The price of living the retired lifestyle you want is another factor.

Visit the government website to learn how much of a State Pension you will receive.

Your pension choices are:

If you decide to retire early, you must decide on your pension money.

If your pension is a defined contribution, you can withdraw as much as you choose from it.

You can withdraw up to one-fourth tax-free. The remainder will be taxed.

A gradual retirement

Many people prefer to retire gradually rather than stop their jobs entirely.

You might be able to take out a smaller portion of your pension now and a larger one later under your employer's plan.
Otherwise, you might wish to think about moving to a personal pension of your choosing.

So if transferring would require giving up a particularly lucrative pension or guarantees, proceed with caution.

Another choice is to accept your employer's offer of early retirement and then hunt for another employment, perhaps one that is part-time.

Planning for a pension can be challenging. Before making any significant decisions, it's crucial to consult an impartial financial consultant if you're unsure of what to do.

Redundancy alternatives include:

An alternative to being laid off can be working fewer hours.

These are five actions you should do if early retirement is one of your goals:

Retirement Preparation

Early retirement before age 65 and the freedom — and other benefits — that comes with it may be the most typical cubicle daydream.
Nonetheless, you can be forced by life to retire earlier than you had anticipated.
Here is all the information you need to prepare for early retirement, regardless of the situation.

What is the age of early retirement?

Early retirement is sometimes defined by those who pursue it as retiring in their 40s, 50s, or even sooner.

Some want to retire so they may travel, devote time to side projects, or just stop working altogether.

The FIRE movement—which stands for financial independence and early retirement—is frequently used to describe this.

Early retirement has largely been redefined by the FIRE movement, which emphasizes financial independence over simply quitting your job.

Ironically, though, retiring early means putting in a lot of labour because you must finance your retirement because the earliest age at which you can begin receiving Social Security benefits is 62.

But, if you begin receiving Social Security benefits before reaching the full retirement age of 66 or 67, depending on the year you were born, your monthly income will reduce.

Depending on how close you are to the full retirement age, the monthly drop in your payments might result in a cut of up to 30% of your Social Security benefits.

Five steps to an early retirement

1. Modify your budget as it is currently.

Here's where the True work starts:
Regardless of how you look at it, retiring early requires making some adjustments to the way you now make and spend money so that you can enjoy your retirement.

And for many people, that entails spending only what is necessary.

Many people who want to retire early desire to survive on 50% of their salary (or less).
The remainder is put toward savings.

FIRE enthusiasts use a variety of tactics to reduce their expenditure to this level, from the obvious to the absurd.
Eliminating debt is essential, as is reducing both large and small expenses. This includes debt that has traditionally been viewed as "good," like mortgage loans.
Consider innovative ways to reduce the cost of your accommodation, utilities, food, and transportation.
Do you own a bicycle?
Prepare to ride it now.

Finding ways to earn more money that can go directly into your early retirement savings is also a good idea.
There are several FIRE supporters groups, but there are three main ones:

The fat FIRE group and the lean FIRE group, seek to live as healthfully as possible. FIRE advocates who follow the fat model put more emphasis on boosting their income through investments or side jobs so they can retire earlier and live comfortably.

There is also barista FIRE, which emphasizes saving enough money to retire and work whenever and wherever it is comfortable for the individual.

Don't get rid of the car just yet if that sounds better to you.

When you start driving with Lyft, you'll need it.

2. Estimate your yearly retirement expenses

The good news is that you're probably accustomed to making do with a little amount of your income after Step 1.

The presumption that you will continue to do so results in a reduction in the amount of money required for retirement.

Create a retirement expense estimate to demonstrate your point.

To do that, examine your present monthly spending and decide what will decrease, what might increase, and what might be added to or completely deleted.

Your yearly retirement needs are determined by adding up your final monthly spending projections and multiplying by 12.

We'd advise raising it by 10% to 20% to give you some wiggle room and make it spectacular.

You never know when you'll feel like treating yourself to a new haircut.

Taxes and health insurance are two items that are usually forgotten during this calculation and both of which could put an early end to your early retirement.

Particularly for those who obtain their health insurance through employment before retirement, health care is a significant challenge in many arrangements. You have to leave that job and your policy behind.

Alternatives for replacing it include:

The simple option if you're married and your spouse is still employed is to sneak into their schedule.

If not, think about getting private insurance or using Healthcare.gov to look for a plan.

You might also look for part-time jobs with health insurance—some employers give it to such workers—or check to see whether you qualify for group coverage through an industry association.

The last choice should be COBRA, a pricey method of temporarily continuing your employer-provided insurance while paying all of the payments yourself.

Finally, we will discuss everyone's topic: taxes.
As always, reducing them is the main objective.
You'll need to plan how and when to withdraw money from your investment accounts to do that.

Remember that there are frequent restrictions on when you can take qualifying distributions from tax-advantaged retirement plans like 401(k)s and IRAs, with the majority of them needing a minimum age of 5912 to avoid taxes and penalties.
(Roth IRAs are an exception; you can distribute contributions at any time, but not earnings.)

The early distribution guidelines have a few exceptions.

One strategy that is common among early retirees is to begin a series of roughly equal periodic payments, which the IRS will permit as long as you adhere to certain guidelines.

Consider working with a financial consultant to create a plan for drawing from your investments while avoiding penalties and taxes, if possible.

3. Calculate your overall savings requirements.

Thanks to a handful of general guidelines that early retirees frequently adhere to, the work you performed to define your expenditures has already put you halfway through this one.

The first is the "rule of 25": Before retiring, you should have 25 times your anticipated yearly expenses saved.

As a result, if you anticipate spending $30,000 in your first year of retirement, you should have $750,000 invested when you quit your job.

As a result of inflation, the rule assumes that your retirement savings are invested to grow over time. After all, your spending will rise every year, at least somewhat, and your investments must reflect this.

The 4% rule, which states that you can withdraw 4% of your invested savings during your first year of retirement, brings us to the second rule.

After that, you receive that sum with an inflation adjustment.

The 4% rule was developed as a result of studies done in the 1990s that compared different withdrawal tactics to previous market situations.

Depending on your investments, risk tolerance, and the state of the market when you retire, you might wish to adopt a more or less cautious strategy.

Yet there is still this caveat: Neither of these guidelines is infallible.
Finding a financial advisor that would promise your results is difficult.
Yet, they are typically regarded as sound tactics.

If you intend to rely on funds from tax-deferred retirement accounts, keep in mind that taking withdrawals before age 591/2, which is considered early retirement, may result in income taxes and penalties.
But, there are no time limits on when you can withdraw money from a brokerage account.

4. Invest in the expansion

At the risk of stating the obvious, retiring early implies you have a longer period during which your savings must support your spending and a shorter period during which they can.

Both of those statements imply that investment returns will be your best ally.
You must invest in a diversified portfolio focused on long-term growth to get the best results.
For as long as you can handle it, think about investing in low-cost index funds with a stock-heavy allocation.

You might believe the contrary to be true: You should take less risk since you have less time left before retiring.
However, it's crucial to keep in mind that the period you spend in retirement should be included in that horizon. You may be retired for 50 or 60 years, in which case you'll need your money to continue to grow.

As you get closer to your anticipated retirement date, you should probably move a small portion of your assets into safer, more liquid havens so you can access them without having to worry about losing money on investments.

Maybe you use a year or two's worth of costs for that.

The remainder, however, should be kept invested and gradually converted to cash as needed, allowing your money to grow and supporting the 4% distribution rate that was previously mentioned.

5. Keep an eye on your spending

You've put in a reasonable lot of effort in predicting your retirement expenses.

The more difficult task will be keeping to that estimate.

You give yourself a retirement party as a little first step.

Then, with some spare time on your hands (remember, you're retired), you decide to take a trip, aimlessly peruse the mall, learn to prepare fine cuisine, or purchase a dog.

That 4% has a one in front of it all of a sudden.

Not to be obvious, but the 4% rule only functions if you follow it.

It's intended to support small increases in spending up to the rate of inflation, but not much more.

The risk of running out of money rises with each increase in spending, especially recurring costs like a new debt payment.

Running out of money typically results in returning to work for most people, but we'll say it regardless.

CHAPTER 2

Retirement Risks

Technically, Grant Sabatier, the founder of the finance website Millennial Money and the author of "Financial Freedom," is still working.
Though he might be.
He doesn't need to work again because he has enough money in his portfolio to support himself.
Because in a way, that is the key point.

Sabatier is a prominent proponent of the so-called FIRE movement, which stands for financial independence and early retirement.
To have enough money to retire decades before they reach their mid-60s, adherents of this concept try to save and invest

significant percentages of their income during their early earning years.

At the age of 30, Sabatier had amassed enough savings to guarantee his retirement with $1.25 million by 2015.

However, he has started a new business teaching people how to become financially independent instead of relaxing on a beach.

Sabatier has witnessed his fair share of FIRE success stories over the past eight years, as well as typical snares that early retirees encounter.

According to Sabatier, there are two major trouble areas you should be aware of today if you're thinking of starting a FIRE adventure to avoid them later.

1. It's risky to retire before developing a post-career identity.

Preparing for an early retirement necessitates having a sense of what life will be like after work, which can be challenging in a culture where individuals are frequently defined by their jobs.

According to Sabatier, "so much of our identity is connected to our work and the things we accomplish in our professional life."

Many people put in a lot of effort working, saving, and investing to retire early, but they often don't know what they want to do afterwards.

Knowing how much money to set aside can be challenging since different financial scenarios—such as retiring to a beach in Thailand, working on your novel in a café, or driving across the country in a van—require varying amounts of savings.

Concentrating on your basic principles is one method to make decisions more focused.

Jim Crider, a licensed financial adviser who focuses on clients seeking financial independence, recently told CNBC that, asking an aspiring retiree which aspects of his life make him the happiest being, might help him to get a better picture of what he wants.

"Your vision is clear if you can be eloquent about what's essential to you," he stated.
"Money can be spent in the most effective way possible.
The things that are most essential to you can be accomplished in a grander, more impressive manner.

But, Sabatier cautions that even if your retirement vision is crystal clear, some field testing may be necessary.
Try a "mini-retirement" if you have enough cash saved up to cover a year or more of costs to get a feel for life away from the office, he advises.

Or start part-time passion projects while you're still employed.

"Starting a side business will allow you to start earning money doing something you enjoy, and this is one of the main reasons I advise doing so.

Use that as a transition to early retirement when you decide to do so.

2. Underestimating the amount necessary to retire

If you don't put enough money away, none of your early retirement goals is likely to come true.

"I see a lot of individuals retiring with enough money to pay their annual expenses today," says Sabatier, "but they're not considering what adding two kids or moving to a higher cost of living location could contribute to their spending."

The amount of money that early retirees need in their portfolio to support themselves indefinitely is referred to as their "FIRE number" and is what they are aiming towards.

The formula used to determine it is based on the "4% rule," an investment principle that emerged from a significant financial study published in 1998 that suggested investors holding a combination of stocks and bonds might remove 4% of the value of their portfolio annually.

If you estimate a 4% withdrawal rate, you would multiply the annual income you anticipate you'll require in retirement by 25 to determine your FIRE number.
To retire on $50,000 a year in withdrawals from their assets, a person would require $1.25 million.

According to Sabatier, when people fail to take into consideration how that equation may change for them over time, they put themselves in difficulty.

When you started your FIRE adventure in your 20s, you might have felt $50,000 was plenty to get by, but by the time you're 45, your needs might have significantly changed.

Before you can enjoy the retirement you had in mind, you may need to raise your number.

You might need to revise your expectations about when you might reach your goal as well, Sabatier says.

That's because it's based on the notion that markets will steadily climb upward to safely withdraw your capital.

Although that has been the general pattern for a very long time, the direction of your investments between now and the time you hope to retire is far less predictable.

"We are aware that the world is becoming more unstable.
I notice that many people underestimate their ability to save and overestimate the stock market's possible future performance.

Early retirement is one of the worst financial mistakes, according to a Harvard-trained economist. Here's why you'll "regret" it:

Pulling my punches is not in my DNA as an economist.
I'll be direct, then:
Early retirement is one of the worst financial mistakes that most Americans will later regret; it's not just a choice to take the longest vacation of their lives.

The explanation is straightforward: Because we collectively are bad savers, early retirement is unaffordable.

Financially speaking, retiring later is typically far safer and a lot wiser.

Half of today's working families run the risk of having their standard of living significantly fall in retirement, according to a Boston College Center for Retirement Research report.
If all workers retired two years later, the percentage would decrease by about 50%.

Naturally, there are circumstances in which retiring early is a fantastic choice.
Some folks have properly thought out their finances and can purchase more leisure.
Many people are powerless; they exhaust their physical or mental resources.
In some cases, jobs are mechanized or outsourced.

Nonetheless, despite having saved virtually nothing, between the ages of 57 and 66, approximately two-thirds of persons decide to retire early of their own free will.

Furthermore, the majority of them are healthy and free of conditions that would make it impossible for them to continue working.

The catastrophe of baby boomer retirement

Consider the 76 million-strong baby boomer generation, who are retiring in large numbers. They were born between 1946 and 1964.

A little under half of them have any savings at all.

They have a median wealth of only $144,000, which is less than three years' worth of average household spending.

Things would be better if they had sizable private, public, or local pensions to rely on.

Not at all.

Notwithstanding Social Security, fewer than one-third of people have a pension.
Regarding individuals who received pensions, many worked for municipal and state governments, which are not covered by Social Security.

Worst yet, due to Social Security's Windfall Elimination and Government Pension Offset rules, persons receiving such pensions risk losing the majority of their Social Security benefits accumulated while working a part-time job in a covered occupation.

The average Social Security payment is $18,000 per year, which might be far higher, but 94% of retirees begin receiving Social Security retirement benefits well before the benefit cap of age 70.

In actuality, about 85% should hold off on collecting until they are 70.

When adjusted for inflation, the retirement payout at age 70 is 76% more than the benefit at age 62, for instance.

Also, by taking their Social Security retirement benefits much too early, Americans risk depriving their current or former spouses (whom they were married to for ten years or longer) of much lesser widow(er) and divorced widow(er) payments.

You can't plan for your death.

Most of us don't save, which is a reflection of a misplaced emphasis on life expectancy, which is frequently used to determine one's planning horizon.

By age 50, 50% of people will survive past the age of 80.

A quarter of people will live to be 90.

Take Jane, a 40-year-old single Louisianan, as an example to better understand what appropriate saving entails.

Jane makes $75,000 per year and has $150,000 in her savings account thanks to an inheritance from a wealthy uncle. She intends to retire and start collecting Social Security at the age of 62.

Jane might reach 100 years old.

Like the rest of us, Jane cannot plan on passing away when it is expected.

She needs to make plans to live as long as she can since she might.

Jane has no savings.

She is relying on Social Security and her 401(k), which has a $150,000 balance and receives 3% yearly contributions from both her workplace and herself, to support her retirement.

Jane is far from the mark.

She might retire after more time than she spends working.

She needs to put aside 28% of her annual income through retirement if she lives to 100!

What if Jane enrols in Social Security at age 70?

a wise move!

As a result, her lifetime spending goes up by more than 10% and her required pre-retirement saving rate drops to 16%.

And what if she bets on dying soon and decides to cut her standard of life starting at the age of 80 by 1.5% annually?

Her necessary savings rate is now 13%.

Jane is regrettably not saving anything.

If she keeps acting in this way, her standard of living after retirement will be half what it was before!

Jane, though, is in better physical condition than most.
A third of employees in the private sector do not have a retirement plan.
Moreover, 25% of those who do participate stop before receiving their free employer match.

The solution is to put off retiring.

How can Jane's retirement be saved when she can't?
Jane won't need to save on her own if she retires at 70 and begins receiving Social Security.
Also, her lifetime expenditure will increase by 30%!

This is a hazardous tactic, no doubt.
Jane might develop a disability.
Or, she might be let go.
She can only continue working if she doesn't want to suffer from serious financial

hardship in retirement and doesn't want to save a lot of money.

CHAPTER 3:

Seven Strategies to Be More Prepared for Medical Costs in Retirement.

According to the most recent Consumer Spending Survey, healthcare expenses for seniors come in at number three behind prescription medicines, health insurance, and medical services and supplies.
Retirement families spend, on average, $562 per month ($6,749) on healthcare.
Health insurance makes up the majority of this expenditure.

The bad news is that healthcare costs will probably continue to rise even more quickly than they have in the past. According to the Centers for Medicare & Medicaid Services, healthcare costs will increase at a 2.5% annual rate over the next ten years as a result of healthcare inflation and the fact that people are living longer.

As a result, according to a recent Fidelity study, a typical couple turning 65 today may need to spend roughly $300,000 in after-tax funds to pay for healthcare costs in retirement.

Long-term care is not even factored into that sum.

There is good news?

Planning will make it less likely that your retirement costs will be significantly impacted by healthcare costs.

Here are seven strategies (given in no particular order) to help you better budget for medical costs.

1. Benefit from catch-up contributions

The IRS permits "catch-up contributions" every year after you turn 50.

These are additional contributions to your 401(k) and IRA that you can make over the usual annual limits.
This option is available to promote saving and lessen the financial strain of retirement.

You should take advantage of the benefit since the tax-deferred growth might greatly increase your retirement savings if it makes sense in your overall strategy.
As of 2021, you are permitted to contribute $13,500 to a SIMPLE 401(k) and $19,500 to a 401(k) (k).
You can add an extra $6,500 to a 401(k) account through catch-up contributions, as well as an extra $3,000 for SIMPLE 401(k) accounts.
The combined contribution for traditional and Roth IRAs in 2021 is $6,500.
You can add an extra $1,000 with catch-up contributions.

2. Postpone receiving your Social Security benefits.

Your monthly benefit amount will depend on when you choose to start receiving Social Security benefits (you can start as early as age 62).
You will get a permanent cut in your monthly payment if you decide to start receiving benefits before you reach full retirement age, which is the age at which you first become eligible for full Social Security benefits.

More specifically, from the time you turn 62 to the time you reach full retirement age, Social Security benefits rise by around 7% annually.
Between your full retirement age and age 70, the increase thereafter is roughly 8% annually.

As an example, let's say you wait until your full retirement age and receive the entire $1,000 a month in Social Security benefits. Your benefit will be reduced by about 30% to $700 if you apply for benefits at age 62.

As you can see, if you start collecting too soon, you could lose out on thousands of dollars in benefits each year that could be used to pay for healthcare costs.

3. Investigate your alternatives for long-term care.

Experts advise getting long-term care coverage (either separately or through your life insurance policy) in your mid to late fifties to lock in a reduced premium, though every person's circumstance is unique, especially if you have a family history of illness at an early age.

There are various causes for this, but the main one is that you must meet the requirements for long-term care insurance eligibility, which necessitates good health to purchase coverage.

As many people begin to notice a minor decline in their health in their 50s, it seems sensible that 24% of those between the ages of 60 and 64 who applied for long-term care in 2019 had their applications declined.

This percentage rose to about 33% for those between the ages of 65 and 69, and it dramatically rose for those aged 70 and older.

Long-term care premiums are determined by the age at which you apply, which is another reason to purchase insurance when you're younger.

Yet, since more than 95% of long-term insurance claims are made by persons aged 70 or older, you don't want to buy a policy too soon.

In other words, if you purchase a policy in your 40s, you probably won't need to claim for another 20 years or more.

You should at least plan for long-term care if you don't want to pay for a policy (we know they aren't cheap). This is especially important given the costs.

Home health aides cost an average of $4,385, assisted living facilities cost $4,051, and nursing homes with individual rooms cost $8,517 per month nationwide, according to multiple sources.

Also, between 2004 and 2019, the cost of long-term care increased by an average of 1.71% to 3.64% per year.

Having the plan to account for these costs is therefore essential.

4. Take into consideration, a health savings account

You can utilize a Health Savings Account (HSA), a type of savings account, to cover deductibles and other eligible out-of-pocket medical costs.

Even though these accounts were created primarily to assist individuals with high-deductible health insurance plans (HDHP), they can be a great tool to save for future medical costs since account balances can roll over each year.

A further $1,000 in "catch-up" payments may be made to the account once you turn 55.

5. Know your Medicare alternatives.

Medicare Part B and Part D premiums are thought to account for over 40% of a retiree's medical expenses.

Hence, to maximize advantages and prevent expensive Medicare blunders, it's necessary to have more than just a basic awareness of how the program operates.

Taking Medicare Advantage or Medigap plans into account may be beneficial.

While not suitable for everyone, these supplemental and alternative plans may help you avoid paying out-of-pocket costs.

6. Put money into a life insurance policy.

A permanent life insurance policy is one approach to augment your retirement savings, even though it is not inexpensive, as these plans often allow you to accrue cash value in addition to your death benefit (paid by a percentage of your premiums).

An insurance policy with cash value can be compared to an investment-like savings account with a death benefit.

One benefit is that you can take money out of the cash value/savings you've built whenever you need to and spend it as you like.

Accelerated death benefit (sometimes known as "living benefits") riders are available on the majority of permanent life insurance policies, and more recently, many term policies.

Whether you are terminally, severely, or chronically ill, these policy clauses allow you to receive benefits while you are still alive (sometimes known as "living benefits").

The financial pressures you and your family may be under could be lessened by these perks.

7. Engage in physical activity

A brisk 30-minute walk is a good example of the kind of activity that can lower blood pressure, keep your bones, muscles, and joints healthy, ease depression or anxiety symptoms, lower your risk of heart disease, and help you better manage chronic conditions like diabetes and arthritis, according to several sources, including WebMD.

In conclusion, ways to prepare for growing healthcare expenditures

Although you may be in good condition right now, it is impossible to anticipate your state of health when you retire.
So, it is advisable to plan so that any unexpected medical costs don't negatively affect your finances and way of life in retirement.

CHAPTER 4

HOW TO COPE WITH INADEQUATE SAVINGS BEFORE RETIREMENT

Although it may not be ideal, this represents the hard reality for many Americans.

What might retirement look like without savings?

That question is not as absurd as it might appear.

According to a 2019 Northwestern Mutual report, 15% of American people have no retirement savings at all, while 22% have less than $5,000 saved for their golden years.

According to the same survey, consumers generally believe there is a 45% probability they will outlive their investments.

That's not the best-case situation.

KEY LESSONS

Saving for retirement is more important than ever because it could last for 20 years or longer.

You could need to reduce your house or scale back your lifestyle if you don't have enough retirement savings.

Many elderly people who don't have enough money for retirement may need to work part-time jobs if they can.

What Takes Place If Retirement Savings Aren't Made?

Having a nest fund is crucial since retirement signifies the end of a reliable income stream.

Once you stop working, you can require up to 80% of your pre-retirement income.

Hence, if your annual income while employed was $100,000, you will need up to $80,000 annually to support your lifestyle after leaving the employment.

You would have to continue working or drastically reduce your spending if you didn't have any savings or a pension plan (both are uncommon).

For many people who don't have any savings when they retire, Social Security becomes their sole source of income.

According to the Center on Budget and Policy Priorities, 20% of seniors depend on it for 90% or more of their income, while 50% of seniors receive 50% or more of their income from it.

In the past, a large number of employees relied on business pension schemes to fully or largely support their retirement.

These plans, though, are getting harder to find.

There is still certain government employment that offers pensions, but it's crucial to remember that the profits from those positions could not have had Social Security taxes deducted, which could reduce your Social Security payment.

Largely reliant on Social Security?

For retirees who were used to earning much more, the average monthly Social Security retirement benefit check of $1,509 as of June 2021 can come as a major shock.

An average retiree's pre-retirement wages are only replaced by Social Security to the extent of 40%.

Even while there are ways to make the most of it, social security still works best as a supplement to individual savings.

Living exclusively (or largely) off of Social Security may not be feasible when you take into account healthcare costs like Medicare payments, essential living costs like food and shelter, personal debt, and other financial obligations many seniors have.

You might have to alter your way of life.

It will be challenging to live the same lifestyle in retirement as you had while working if you don't have any money.

You might need to make changes, such as downsizing your house or apartment, giving up luxuries like cable television, an iPhone, or a gym membership, or driving a more affordable vehicle.

Many seniors find that moving to a smaller home is insufficient.

They must dispose of their properties and relocate with their grown children.

One expects that the sale of a house will yield a healthy nest egg even without the need to buy a new residence.

Perhaps getting a roommate is necessary.

Seniors who still own homes and have not saved more money for retirement may use their residences as a source of income.

Some people may decide to do this by renting out a portion of their home as a separate apartment.

Others might end up getting a roommate as a result.

Both have potential dangers.

Being a landlord is good if you don't mind sharing space, but renting a room could be a harsh pill to take if you're the kind of retiree who loves peace and doesn't want to share.

A reverse mortgage on a home is another choice, however, doing so can be expensive and difficult.

You might need to keep doing part-time jobs.

You may require an additional income source in retirement to cover your basic expenses.
This can entail returning to work or securing a part-time position.
Seniors can work remotely more easily than ever thanks to the Internet.
Due to their propensity for dependability and loyalty, retailers are likewise eager to hire retirees.
Yet, not all elders can work, particularly those with poor health.

It may not even be possible to retire.

Retirement may not be an option for you at all if you haven't saved any money for it and aren't willing to change your way of life, especially if Social Security isn't enough to support you.

The main reason why many people choose to postpone retirement and continue working is that they don't have enough money saved.

The summary is this:

Without savings, retiring would involve significant sacrifices.

Retirement with Social Security as your single source of income will demand significant modifications because most people cannot sustain their pre-retirement lifestyles on that amount of money.

Making those adjustments and even continuing to work part-time will be sufficient for some people to support themselves.

Others will have to forgo retirement entirely due to a shortage of retirement funds.

CHAPTER 5

10 Early Retirement Myths No One Told You

The fantasy of quitting your job may be very different from reality.
What you should know is this:

A long road and horizon are depicted in the background, with a wood sign with yellow text pointing in opposite directions that reads "Work" and "Retire."

Even if you adore your job, there are moments when you'd rather be organizing the spice rack than cramming into a crowded train car with a lot of sniffling commuters.
And when you sway in the car next to a man who has biked four hours to the station, you could be considering retiring early.

However, not everyone is a good candidate for early retirement.

It isn't for the majority of people, in reality.

An Employee Benefit Research Institute (EBRI) poll found that only 11% of today's workers intend to retire before age 60.

For many people who do decide to take the risk, early retirement may turn out to be very different from what they had imagined.

Before you decide to retire early, take into account the following.

1. Health care is costly.

Beginning at age 65, Medicare is a government program that offers health insurance to more than 61 million senior citizens.

You'll need a substitute in the interim, and it won't be cheap.

According to Brian Schmehil, director of asset management for the Mather Group in Chicago, private health insurance before Medicare takes effect is quite expensive.

According to current law, your insurance expenses cannot consume more than 8.3 per cent of your household's total income.

A mid-level silver plan would cost $346 per month, or $4,150 annually, for a person with a family income of $50,000, for instance.

2. Using your nest egg prematurely can be expensive.

Most tax-deferred accounts, including traditional IRAs and 401(k) plans, typically have a 10% early withdrawal penalty if you retire before age 59 1/2.

According to Matt Stephens, founder of Wilmington, North Carolina-based Advice

Point, "there are some possibilities for withdrawing IRA funds before age 59 1/2, but it's complex and can result in significant fines if done incorrectly."

Also, if you don't have a Roth IRA, which is funded with after-tax contributions, you'll have to pay income taxes on the money you remove from traditional IRAs that were started with pretax contributions.
For instance, if you take $20,000 from an IRA before reaching age 59 1/2 and you are subject to federal income tax at a rate of 15%, you will be required to pay $5,000 in taxes and penalties, leaving you with only $15,000 in your account.

3. You give up the strength of compound interest

Time is your ally while saving for retirement, but it is not your ally when spending.

If you save $250 per month from the time you are 25 to the time you are 55, that's $3,000 per year. Assuming you don't take any withdrawals and your investments earn an average of 6% per year, you will have about $237,000 when you retire.

Your $90,000 in contributions seem to have yielded a reasonable return.

Let's assume, though, that you continue working for a further ten years before retiring at age 65.

You would have nearly twice as much money, or $464,000, in that case.

Why?

Even though the additional ten years' worth of contributions only totals $30,000, they do assist.

True growth comes from an additional ten years' worth of interest on all the money you contributed as well as interest on the interest that has accumulated for forty years.

4. You could live an extremely long life.

In comparison to a woman retiring at 65, her funds will need to last on average 28.6 years longer if she retires at 55.
A guy must extend his savings for 25.1 years rather than 17.8 if he retires at age 55.
According to the Society of Actuaries, for couples who survive to be 65, there is a 25% chance that the surviving spouse will live to be 98.

According to Angela Dorsey, a certified financial advisor in Torrance, California, "With improved health care, more people are living longer than the national norms."

5. You'll spend more cash than you anticipate.

As a general guideline, you should expect to spend around 80% as much in retirement as you do while working.

After all, if you don't earn any more money, you won't be contributing to your retirement account, driving to work every day, or even contributing to Social Security payroll tax.

But, in the early years of retirement, when you're younger, healthier, and liberated from the restrictions of work, you may very well spend as much as or even more than you did before retirement.

According to a study by J.P. Morgan Asset Management, new retirees typically experience a "spending surge" on travel, home improvements or relocation, and other retirement-related lifestyle changes that level off after two or three years.

Your spending plans may need to be significantly revised given the high 8.6 per cent inflation rate over the past 12 months.

The number of retirees who think their overall expenditures and costs are more than planned has increased from last year to 36%, according to EBRI.

The percentage indicating that particular living and travel costs are more than anticipated rose from the previous year.

According to Sean Pearson, a licensed financial planner from Conshohocken, Pennsylvania, "every day is Saturday."

When you don't have to go to work, you get up and look for stuff to do, which is essentially how we all feel on Saturday.

Certain things may be enjoyable and social.

Work around the house may be necessary at times.

Saturday is frequently the most expensive day of the week because most things require money.

6. Housing cost

Many people who want to retire want to do it without having a mortgage, but few succeed in doing so.

44 per cent of retired homeowners between the ages of 60 and 70 are still paying off their mortgages according to a poll by American Finance.

Even after your mortgage is paid off, you still have additional costs.

According to Dorsey, a financial consultant from California, "home maintenance and rising property taxes might take up a substantial amount of your money."

According to Rocket Mortgage, New Jersey, Illinois, and New Hampshire have the highest property tax rates, while Hawaii, Alabama, and Colorado have the lowest.

As a general rule, homeowners should set aside 1% of the purchase price of their home each year to cover maintenance and replacement costs.

For a $350,000 home, that amounts to $3,500 a year.

Keep in mind that several states provide reduced property tax rates for individuals aged 65 and beyond.

7. It can be challenging to find extra money.

It can be more difficult than you imagine to work in retirement.

Only 27% of actual retirees reported working for compensation, compared to 74% of workers who want to do so after retirement, according to the EBRI research.

Even doing a part-time job might be difficult.

Leslie Beck, a certified financial planner in Rutherford, New Jersey, argues that early retirees don't always recognize that traditional part-time jobs involve a commitment to a schedule that is occasionally not very flexible.

"This could interfere with other retirement plans, like travelling or seeing relatives."

I've seen retirees who were shocked by how rigid part-time work is.

Remember that the earliest you may typically claim retirement benefits is age 62 if you decide to use Social Security to replace the lost income.

Even then, your rewards will be in part.

For those who were born in 1960 or after, the complete retirement age is 67, at which point they are eligible for their entire monthly payment.

The reward amount is decreased by 30% if you file your claim before age 62.

Before going early, here are 5 queries to ask (and respond to).

- Can I afford to quit my job?

- Should I look for a part-time job to make ends meet?

- How can I get medical insurance?

- What will I be doing to pass the time?

- Are my plans in line with those of my spouse or partner?

8. There is a lot of spare time.

You have a 40-hour gap in your week after retirement that you must fill.
In Winchester, Massachusetts, Catherine Valega, a certified financial planner, query clients, "Are you certain you have enough hobbies to keep your body, mind, and spirituality active for the many years you have ahead of you?"

How much time do you envision yourself spending taking strolls, relaxing by the pool, or reading on the couch once the novelty has worn off?

Before retiring, give your decision careful thought.

Do you desire to lend a hand?

Re-Enter the classroom?

Get a new interest or pick up an old one?

Construct a strategy before retiring.

9. You might need to meet new people.

While they still have full-time work, your present friends may not be as accessible if you retire in your 50s.

You have the luxury of going to a matinee or playing a round of golf during the week, but your friends who work 9 to 5 don't.

New friends you make are probably going to be older, according to Dennis Nolte, a certified financial adviser in Oviedo, Florida:

Several of my energetic pre-60-year-old retirees bemoan the fact that their new peer group has different expectations about food, sleep routine, and even cultural references because they are much older than they are.

10. Couples may struggle after retirement.

According to Birmingham, Alabama-based certified financial adviser Patti Black, "retirement is a significant life shift, and you have to be patient with yourself and your partner."

"Most retired couples don't resemble those portrayed in advertisements and commercials,"

You'll need to decide how housework will alter.

Are you going to split the cooking, cleaning, and yard work?

And are you planning to live together round-the-clock, especially if you downgrade to a smaller house?

A marriage may suffer significantly as a result of these choices.
In contrast to all other age groups, Black warns that "grey divorce," or divorce occurring after the age of 50, has increased by half since 1990.
"And the wife is typically the one who files for divorce after age 50."

CONCLUSION

More than ever, you should start saving for retirement because it may last 20 or more years.

Retirement would require considerable sacrifices if there were no funds.
Most people cannot maintain their pre-retirement lives on that amount of

money, so if Social Security is your only source of income in retirement, you will need to make major adjustments.

Some people can support themselves by making those changes and even by continuing to work part-time.

Due to a lack of retirement assets, some people will have to completely fargo retirement.

www.ingramcontent.com/pod-product-compliance
Lightning Source LLC
Chambersburg PA
CBHW071140220526
45467CB00015B/1636